JOHN TYLER

PRESIDENTIAL ✦ LEADERS

JOHN TYLER

KATE HAVELIN

LERNER PUBLICATIONS COMPANY/MINNEAPOLIS

To my mother, Marie Havelin, whose idea of a great vacation
was visiting homes of the presidents. This one's for you, Mom.

Lerner Publications Company
A division of Lerner Publishing Group
241 First Avenue North
Minneapolis, MN 55401 U.S.A.

Website address: www.lernerbooks.com

Library of Congress Cataloging-in-Publication Data

Havelin, Kate, 1961–
    John Tyler / Kate Havelin.
        p.   cm. — (Presidential leaders)
    Includes bibliographical references and index.
    ISBN: 0–8225–1395–1 (lib. bdg. : alk. paper)
        1. Tyler, John, 1790–1862—Juvenile literature. 2. Presidents—United States—Biography—
Juvenile literature. I. Title. II. Series.
    E397.H385 2005
    973.5'8'092—dc22   2004004707

Manufactured in the United States of America
1 2 3 4 5 6 – JR – 10 09 08 07 06 05

CONTENTS

———————— ✧ ————————

News that arrived by letter on April 5, 1841, changed Vice President John Tyler's life forever.

INTRODUCTION

He [John Tyler] is a slave-monger [slave owner] whose talents are not above mediocrity. No one ever thought of his being placed in the executive [president's] chair.

—John Quincy Adams

On a sunny April afternoon in 1841, Vice President John Tyler was on his hands and knees, playing marbles with his eleven-year-old son, Tazewell, when a young man on horseback sped toward their mansion in Williamsburg, Virginia. "See what the ruckus is about, Taze," Tyler told his son.

The horseback rider was Fletcher Webster, chief clerk in the U.S. secretary of state's office. Webster's father, Daniel, was the U.S. secretary of state. Fletcher Webster rushed to tell his news: "I have been instructed by the Secretary of State to deliver this dispatch [news] to you without an instant's delay."

Tyler quickly scanned Webster's letter. "O Lord! How did it happen? Is it true that Harrison is dead so soon?" Tyler asked.

"Yes, sir, Mr. President," Webster answered. "Washington is now in mourning, you are requested to go—dressed just as you are now."

With that, John Tyler and Fletcher Webster hurried to make their way back to Washington, D.C. Just a month earlier, William Henry Harrison had been sworn in as president of the United States. With Harrison's sudden death, his vice president, John Tyler, would be the new president.

No one knows if that story is true. Another version is that Fletcher Webster arrived in Williamsburg around sunrise on April 5, when the Tyler family was still asleep. Webster supposedly woke up the vice president and told him that Harrison had died and that he, John Tyler, was president.

There's no record of how Tyler reacted when he learned that the president had died. But it's likely that Harrison's death came as a shock. The vice president didn't know that Harrison was sick with pneumonia. Without telephones, the Internet, radios, TVs, or telegraphs, and just a few railroads, news spread slowly. The first official notice that Harrison was sick was in the March 31, 1841, *National Intelligencer* newspaper. The newspaper ran a brief item saying that the president was feeling better. Back then, vice presidents didn't live in Washington or work closely with their presidents. Instead, vice presidents attended key events such as the inauguration and sessions of Congress but then went back to their private homes.

Harrison, at the age of sixty-eight, had been the oldest elected president. His age had been mentioned during the election, but it didn't stop voters from choosing him as their leader. In contrast, Tyler, at fifty-one, was about to

*At his home in Virginia, Tyler (right) receives
the news that President Harrison has died.*

─────────────── ✧ ───────────────

become the youngest U.S. president. No one knew what kind of leader he would be, and few people had considered that he might become president.

When Tyler took over, many people assumed he would be temporary. They expected him to be a caretaker, an acting president. But John Tyler didn't consider himself an acting president. Once William Henry Harrison died, Tyler viewed himself as the rightful president. He refused to open mail addressed to "Hon. John Tyler, Acting President." He hated being called "His Accidency," the nickname given him by his political rival, Senator Henry Clay of Kentucky. Although many Americans did consider Tyler to be an accidental president, he came from a family with a history of power and leadership.

CHAPTER ONE

A PRIVILEGED LIFE

He was so frank and generous, so social and cordial... that you were ready to give him your hand and heart in return for his, which he seemed ever ready to proffer.

—George Wythe Munford,
clerk of the Virginia House of Delegates, mid-1800s

John Tyler was born in Charles City County, Virginia, on March 29, 1790, to one of the most influential families in the state. Tyler's ancestor, Henry Tyler, came to Virginia from Great Britain in the mid-1700s and quickly acquired key pieces of property. Henry's son was among those who helped build the city of Williamsburg. The Tyler family claimed to be a part of history since the eleventh century, when a Tyler supposedly accompanied the English king, William the Conqueror, from France to England.

John's father, Judge John Tyler, served three terms as Virginia's governor before becoming a judge. His mother,

Mary Amistead Tyler, was the daughter of a prominent Virginia plantation owner.

The Tylers weren't wealthy by modern standards, but they owned several plantations, including one called Greenway, on a rich section of land bounded by the James and York rivers. The area was home to many of the state's most prominent people, who were known as the First Families of Virginia.

LIFE AT GREENWAY

John Tyler grew up on a lovely 1,200-acre estate. Its driveway was lined with cedar and willow trees. Judge Tyler described Greenway as a "genteel, well-furnished dwelling . . . surrounded by outbuildings, including a study, storehouse, kitchen, laundry, dairy, meat house, icehouse,

———————————— ✧ ————————————

In Charles City County, Virginia, this graceful home, called Greenway, was John Tyler's birthplace and childhood home. He lived there again as an adult with his wife, Letitia, and their children for about twenty years.

barn, two granaries, two carriage houses, twenty stalls for horses . . . general quarters [and] slave quarters." The Greenway plantation had fields of wheat, corn, and tobacco, all maintained by more than forty slaves.

John was the sixth of eight Tyler children growing up at Greenway. One week after John's seventh birthday, his mother died of a stroke. Some people believe John Tyler grew to depend heavily on his father's opinions. Judge Tyler was not easy to impress.

At school John had a strict teacher, a Mr. McMurdo. Young John thought the Scotsman McMurdo was so mean that "it was a wonder that he did not whip all the sense out of his scholars." One day when John was ten, he and

——————————— ✧ ———————————

When John was young, schoolteachers were expected to be tough on students. Classes were small and often crowded into just one room.

his classmates revolted. They tied McMurdo's hands and feet, then left school with their schoolmaster locked inside the classroom.

After a passerby freed McMurdo, the angry teacher went to John Tyler's father, demanding that John be punished for leading the class rebellion. When Tyler's father heard the facts, he sided with his son, saying, "Sic Semper Tyrannis!" That Latin phrase, which is Virginia's state motto, means loosely, "This is what happens to tyrants."

John wasn't a wild child, but that story shows some of the steel hiding inside the mild-mannered schoolboy with the "slender frame . . . silky brown hair, a bright blue eye, a merry mischievous smile and silver laugh." Even as a child, John wasn't afraid to take on the powerful.

The Virginia State Seal—with the Latin motto John's father quoted to McMurdo—was designed in 1776.

But much of the time, Judge Tyler was more apt to find fault with his son. "I can't help telling you how much I am mortified to find no improvement in your handwriting," the judge wrote his son. "Neither do you connect your lines straight, which makes your letters look abominable. It is an easy thing to correct this fault, and unless you do how can you be fit for law business of every description?"

The judge probably wrote that letter when John was thirteen. That's when he went away to school to start preparing for college. Like his father, John went to William and Mary College in Williamsburg. The school had a history of its students going on to hold important positions in the country. Judge Tyler's college roommate was a fellow Virginian—Thomas Jefferson—who later became the country's third president.

At William and Mary, John studied Greek and Roman literature and history, played the violin, and graduated shortly after his seventeenth birthday. He was a good enough student to win the right to give the commencement address. After college, John studied law. Before he turned twenty, he had a license to practice law, like his father. He was too young to be admitted to Virginia's bar, the state's official association of lawyers. But the examining judge who gave John his license didn't ask his age. So John Tyler was ready to begin earning a living.

LAW AND LOVE

Tyler became known as an eloquent defense attorney who could make impassioned speeches for his clients. The six-foot-tall southerner with the slender build and long,

*After leaving Mr. McMurdo's classroom, Tyler attended
William and Mary College in Williamsburg, Virginia.
He graduated from the college in 1807.*

narrow nose had a silver tongue—a smooth way of speaking. By all accounts, he was a popular and successful
lawyer.

At twenty-one, Tyler was elected to the Virginia House
of Delegates, the state's government, where he would serve
five years. When the War of 1812 between the United
States and Great Britain erupted, Tyler became a captain
of the state militia (part-time citzen's army), but he never
saw battle. After the war ended in 1815, he quickly
returned to his life of law and government. As his political
career blossomed, so did his personal life. While studying
law, he had met Letitia Christian, a shy woman his age

Both Letitia Christian (above) and Tyler were twenty-three years old when they married.

who was the daughter of a wealthy Virginia family. The couple courted for five years. They exchanged portraits, and Tyler sent Letitia love sonnets that he had written. Tyler said he never asked Letitia for a kiss until three weeks before their wedding. They married in 1813, on Tyler's twenty-third birthday.

Shortly after the Tylers wed, Letitia's parents died. The young couple received a large inheritance from them. Letitia's money and social position helped Tyler build his career. By the time he was twenty-seven, Tyler was earning two thousand dollars a year, a reasonable income at the time. He had just been elected to the U.S. House of Representatives, becoming one of the youngest members of Congress.

STATES' RIGHTS

Tyler's first speech in Congress ripped into what was known as the Salary Grab Act, a plan to increase lawmakers' pay to $1,500 a year, more than doubling it. Tyler's firm opposition won him praise back home. At reelection time, his supporters got out the vote, bringing to the polls, "the maimed, the halt [people who limp], the blind, and those who had never voted for anyone." Tyler received all but one of the two hundred votes in Charles City County, the area he represented.

From the beginning of his career in politics, Tyler stood firm on the rights of states to make their own laws. He didn't believe the federal (U.S.) government should be able to create a national bank, raise tariffs (taxes on imports), or even build roads throughout the growing country. Like his father's friend, Thomas Jefferson, John Tyler believed the federal government's power came from what states wanted. Tyler also believed that Congress and the federal government didn't have the power to decide whether newly settled territories should allow slavery.

While Tyler was serving in Congress, Letitia chose to stay back in Virginia. The Tylers had settled in at Greenway, John's childhood home. Letitia managed the estate and cared for their three children, Mary, Robert, and John.

Tyler had health problems while in Washington. He was living in a boardinghouse, where he was served what he called stale fish. The fish gave him stomach problems that would trouble him for the rest of his life. By 1821, when Tyler was thirty-one, he decided not to run for Congress again. Tyler publicly cited his ill health, but he privately wrote to Virginia's governor that he was "tired of Congress and nothing but a strong sense of duty would keep me there." It's likely Tyler was also tired of not making enough money to support his family. His law income had slipped to $1,200, almost half of what he had earned before going to Washington.

———————————————— ✦ ————————————————

"These are sacrifices which it gives me pain to make," Tyler wrote in his 1836 letter of resignation from the U.S. Senate.

Tyler went home to Virginia, where he served once again in the state's House of Delegates before being elected governor, just as his father had been. In 1827 Tyler was appointed a U.S. senator and returned to the nation's capitol.

By January 1833, President Andrew Jackson asked Congress for special power to send miliatry troops to South Carolina to settle a dispute over tariffs. Most southern members of Congress left the capitol in anger over this decision. But Tyler remained in Washington, D.C. and cast the only vote against Jackson's so-called "force bill." Tyler argued that the federal government didn't have the right to use military force against any state.

Later in 1833, Tyler voted to censure, or disapprove of, President Jackson's actions in South Carolina and other matters. By 1836, Tyler had decided to resign from the senate rather than vote to remove the censure vote from Jackson's record.

CHAPTER TWO

TIPPECANOE
AND TYLER TOO

What has caused the great commotion;
motion, motion, our country through?
It is the ball a rolling on.
For Tippecanoe and Tyler Too,
Tippecanoe and Tyler Too
—1840 presidential campaign slogan

John Tyler may have been sick of Congress, but he wasn't
sick of being in government. In 1838, two years after
leaving Washington, D.C., Tyler was back in public office,
once again serving in Virginia's House of Delegates. The
following year, 1839, Tyler decided to run for the U.S.
Senate again, but he ended up tied with the senator in
office, William Rives, another Whig candidate. Back then,
legislators decided whom to send to Congress as their state's
senators. Because of the deadlock over the appointment,
the Virginia legislature postponed its vote on a senator.

Who Were the Whigs?

The Whig Party was a force in U.S. politics from the 1830s to the 1850s. Supporters of Senator Henry Clay and former president John Quincy Adams formed the Whig Party to oppose President Andrew Jackson, a Democrat. Clay and other Whigs believed Jackson was taking too much control of the U.S. government. Most Whigs thought the true power in a democracy should be in Congress, not with the president. The Whigs wanted presidents to serve only one term and not have the right to veto bills. But the Whigs were mainly unified in their distaste for Andrew Jackson, whom they called "King Andrew the First." Whigs believed Jackson was becoming a dictator by seizing too much power for the president.

John Tyler had been a Democrat until he became disgusted by Andrew Jackson's ideas for a strong central government. The Whigs drew southerners like Tyler who believed in states' rights. The Whigs also attracted settlers who wanted to build the West and businesspeople who supported the idea of a national bank. (People like Tyler believed that only individual states had the right to create banks.)

The Whigs won only one presidential election in 1841, when William Henry Harrison was elected president. By the 1850s, the Whigs had split over slavery. Whigs opposed to slaver eventually formed the Republican Party. The name Whig is a shortened version of Whiggamore, a member of a Scottish group that marched to Edinburgh, the capital of Scotland, in 1648 to oppose the official party of the royal court. The British were the first to make Whig a political term.

Later that year, the Whigs instead nominated Tyler to be their vice-presidential candidate on the ticket with William Henry Harrison.

WILLIAM HENRY HARRISON

Harrison, like Tyler, came from a well-established Virginia family. Both men were born in the same area—

✧ ————————

Harrison-Tyler presidential campaign posters could contain a lot of information. This one features portraits of Harrison, Tyler, and two prominent Whig supporters (top); the candidates' biographies (center); battle scenes; and Harrison's home in North Bend, Ohio (bottom).

Charles City County, Virginia. Harrison's father, Benjamin, had signed the Declaration of Independence and, like Tyler's father, had also served as Virginia's governor. Although Harrison grew up in Virginia, he moved west when he was eighteen. He was elected governor of the new Indiana Territory when he was twenty-seven.

As territorial governor, Harrison signed a treaty with Native American leaders that gave settlers about three million acres of land. Not surprisingly, many Native Americans were angry that white people claimed ownership of lands on which Native Americans had lived for many years.

GEN. WILLIAM HENRY HARRISON

Many presidential campaign posters of the 1841 election year focused on Harrison's political career in Indiana Territory.

✧ ─────────────

Two powerful brothers, both tribal chiefs, tried to organize a confederation of tribes from Florida to Canada to stand up to land-hungry settlers. Tecumseh and his brother Tenskwataka, who was known as the Prophet, were determined to protect their people's rights. Governor Harrison and the brothers negotiated for years over disputed lands. Each side threatened and lied to the other. Eventually, in the fall of 1811, Harrison decided to attack.

Harrison and nine hundred soldiers planned to destroy Prophetstown, the Native American capital at the junction of the Wabash and Tippecanoe rivers in Indiana. But on

✧ —————————
Tenskwataka was one of the Native American chiefs who signed a land treaty with Governor Harrison of Indiana Territory.

November 7, 1811, while Tecumseh was away, the Prophet and other Indians attacked Harrison's troops. Many men on both sides died in the fighting. At day's end, Harrison had driven back his attackers and burned Prophetstown.

Settlers praised Harrison for what was generally mis-reported as a U.S. victory at what was known as the Battle of Tippecanoe. Later, during the War of 1812, Harrison, by

———————————— ✧ ————————————

Harrison (seated on horse) *became known as Tippecanoe after burning Prophetstown, a Native American community on the Tippecanoe River in Indiana Territory.*

then a major general in the army, would win a key battle, this one on the Thames River near Detroit (in modern times in Michigan). During the Battle of the Thames, Harrison's troops killed Tecumseh. After that, many Americans considered Harrison a war hero. So in 1839, when it came time to nominate a candidate for president, the Whig Party turned to William Henry Harrison. At the time, Harrison was living on his farm in North Bend, Ohio, where he served as the clerk of the county court.

———————————— ✧ ————————————

Harrison's opponents poked fun at his presidential campaign for emphasizing his military career. They portrayed him as a uniformed puppet in the hands of Senator Henry Clay (left) and Congressman Henry A. Wise of Virginia.

THE POLITICAL DANCING JACK:
A Holiday Gift for Sucking Whigs!!
Sold at No. 104 Nassau, and No. 18 Division Streets, New-York.

The Whig Party chose John Tyler as Harrison's running mate. Although Harrison had grown up in Virginia, he had spent his adult life in the northern regions of Indiana and Ohio. Whig officials thought it was important to have a southerner on the presidential ticket to attract southern voters and others who believed in states' rights, as Tyler did.

PICKING VICE PRESIDENTS

John Tyler became Harrison's vice presidential running mate because the Whig Party wanted a southerner on its ticket. But until 1804, when the Twelfth Amendment to the U.S. Constitution was ratified (passed), political parties didn't get to decide who would be vice president. When the country first began, the candidate who received the most votes in a presidential election became president. The candidate who received the second highest number of votes for president became vice president.

Thomas Jefferson
———— ❖ ————

The U.S. Congress chose to change the way vice presidents were selected after the election of 1800, when Thomas Jefferson *(above)* and Aaron Burr tied for the presidency. The tie forced the U.S. House of Representatives to vote to decide which man would become the third president. They chose Jefferson.

The Whig candidates' names—"Harrison & Tyler"—are printed on the flag flying over the log cabin on this piece of campaign literature from 1841.

LOG CABIN AND HARD CIDER CANDIDATE

The Whig campaign to elect Harrison and Tyler in 1840 broke new ground. For the first time, a presidential candidate actively worked to solicit votes. Few people were interested in the vice-presidential candidate. Tyler made a few speeches late in the campaign, but otherwise, he remained at home.

The campaign was the first to use a catchy slogan—"Tippecanoe and Tyler Too." When a news reporter taunted

Harrison by saying the former military man would be "content to sit in his log cabin and drink hard cider [an inexpensive alcoholic beverage]," the Whigs turned that into a winning theme. They began depicting Harrison as someone who did indeed live in a log cabin and drink hard cider rather than fancy wines. The Whigs said that incumbent (current) president Martin Van Buren was a wealthy man out of touch with common American people.

The Whigs began handing out free whiskey—what they called Whig whiskey—to supporters at their campaign stops. Most of the alcohol came from a liquor distributor from Philadelphia, Pennsylvania, whose name became forever linked with alcohol. The distiller's name was E. G. Booz.

The booze was handed out in bottles shaped like log cabins. Harrison and Tyler's campaign also distributed countless other trinkets—everything from raccoonskin caps to snuffboxes for tobacco, ceramic pitchers and china sets, wooden hairbrushes, belt buckles, and silk ribbons. All the campaign novelties advertised "Tippecanoe and Tyler Too." Voters clamored for the campaign souvenirs.

The Whigs chose to use novelties to promote their candidate, rather than a serious campaign with details about where Harrison and Tyler stood on the issues. Whigs believed letting the candidates talk about issues could cost them votes. Harrison said so little of substance during the campaign that his opponents nicknamed him "General Mum [silent]." Instead of promoting candidate speeches on the issues, the Whigs organized upbeat rallies, which would sometimes last two or three days. The Whigs intended to entertain voters.

CAMPAIGN SONG AND DANCE

Popular culture in the mid-nineteenth century included many forms of musical entertainment. The Whigs popularized campaign songs like this:

> Let Van [Van Buren] from his coolers of silver drink wine
> And lounge on his cushioned settee [sofa];
> Our man on his buckeye [wooden] bench can recline,
> Content with hard cider is he!

Voters bought up campaign novelties like the *Log Cabin Songbook* to learn the words to popular Whig campaign tunes, such as the "Hard Cider Quick Step" and the "Tippecanoe Waltz."

THE TIPPECANOE OR LOG CABIN QUICK STEP.

Composed and respectfully dedicated to

GEN. WILLIAM HENRY HARRISON,

Late A Tippecanoe and Farmer of North Bend.

BY

HENRY SCHMIDT.

BOSTON

Published by HENRY PRENTISS, No 33 Court St.

Businesses as well as voters loved the Harrison-Tyler campaign log cabin and hard cider theme. Publishers eagerly rushed to fill orders for dance music and song sheets *(opposite and above)*. Enterprising businesspeople found many ways to tie their products to the popular politicians. China sets decorated with the candidates' names sold for seven cents per plate. Other products for sale in 1840 included Tippecanoe Tobacco and a skin care product called Log-cabin Emollient.

FEDERAL-ABOLITION-WHIG TRAP.
TO CATCH VOTERS IN.

*This Democratic cartoon warns voters that the Whig campaign
is like an animal trap. Hard cider is the bait and the
log cabin will fall on the voter who takes the bait.*

———————————————— ✧ ————————————————

Whig rallies featured gigantic buckskin-covered balls, up to ten feet in diameter, that Whigs would roll from town to town. The balls were a response to a statement made by Democratic senator Thomas Hart Benton from Missouri, who had claimed he had "started the ball rolling" on a crucial Senate vote. Whigs rolled a huge ball hundreds of miles from Baltimore, Maryland, to Philadelphia. The ball was covered with slogans such as "We need old Tipp to guard the ship." The Whigs' campaign did arouse people's enthusiasm. Thirty thousand people turned out for a Whig parade in Nashville, Tennessee. Almost that many attended a rally in Baltimore. A Whig march in Cincinnati, Ohio, stretched for three miles.

The expression to "keep the ball rolling" printed on this campaign poster, started in the Harrison-Tyler presidential campaign of 1840.

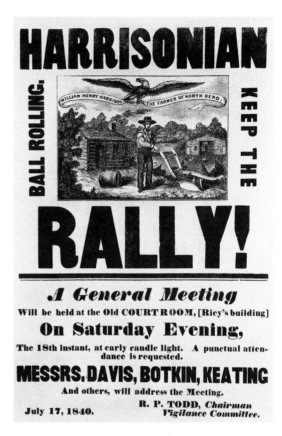

All the gimmicks—from massive slogan balls and raccoonskin caps to log-cabin-shaped liquor bottles—were used to market an upper-class candidate who didn't live in a log cabin and never wore a raccoonskin cap. Harrison had a log cabin on his property, but it had been added onto and wasn't anything like the typical log cabin most settlers had. His family, like that of John Tyler's, had money and power. Harrison's opponents, the Democrats, pointed out that "all this story about the log cabin . . . is a mean fraud." The public didn't seem to know or care.

Neither Harrison nor Tyler discussed the serious problems the country was facing. An economic depression had left many people out of work. At least some citizens were concerned. A group of Pittsburgh Democrats wrote Tyler, asking him whether the country should have a national bank. Tyler wrote that he thought a bank controlled by the federal government was unconstitutional. But

———————————— ✧ ————————————

This political cartoon shows the national bank issue as part of the 1840 presidential race. Democratic presidents Jackson and Van Buren had opposed it. They are portrayed as Uncle Sam's dogs helping Uncle Sam (far left) chase "Mother Bank" as she crawls into Harrison's cider keg.

UNCLE SAM'S PET PUPS!
Or, Mother BANK'S last refuge.
Sold at ELTON'S, 18 Division-Street, New-York.

when he showed the letter to Whig leaders, they told him to avoid controversial subjects. Whigs held Harrison and other top national figures such as Henry Clay to the same deal—avoid serious issues, stick to fluff like log cabin songs and booze.

Election day proved that the Whigs' marketing ploys worked. William Henry Harrison and John Tyler won nineteen of twenty-six states. They carried every big state—except Tyler's home of Virginia, which was still controlled by Democrats. The Whig presidential ticket received 80 percent of all votes, plus an overwhelming number of electoral votes—236—while Van Buren and the Democrats netted just 60.

AFTER VICTORY, WHAT NEXT?

The Whigs' nonstop campaigning had left Harrison exhausted. At the send-off ceremony in his hometown before he left for Washington, the newly elected president told his neighbors, "This may be the last

When Harrison took office, he was already exhausted by all the traveling he had done during the presidential campaign.

time I have the pleasure of speaking to you on earth. I bid you farewell; if forever, fare thee well."

Harrison arrived in Washington, D. C., on February 9, 1841, his sixty-eighth birthday. He was promptly over-whelmed by countless job seekers. He ended up promising the same job to multiple people. "They pursue me so close-ly that I can not even attend to the necessary functions of nature," Harrison complained.

CHILLY INAUGURATION

Bitter winds chilled the nation's capital on March 4, 1841. Harrison's and Tyler's inauguration attracted more specta-tors than any inauguration since George Washington's fifty-two years earlier. In keeping with the Whigs' emphasis on the common man, Harrison rode a horse to the inau-gural, rather than traveling in a covered carriage. Despite cold rains, he wore no coat or hat.

After being sworn in as the ninth president of the United States, Harrison set a record that still stands. He spoke for more than an hour, reading his 8,578-word inauguration speech. By that night, Harrison had a cold. His eyes were watering, and he was coughing. Still, he attended almost every inaugural ball. After the inaugura-tion, Tyler went home to Virginia. He wasn't needed until the Senate was in session later in the year.

Harrison never recovered from that cold. Within the month, it had turned into pneumonia. His last words, spo-ken to the White House physician, seem intended for his vice president. Harrison told his doctor, "Sir, I wish you to understand the true principles of the government. I wish them carried out. I ask nothing more."

A lively crowd gathered at the Capitol for Harrison's inauguration in 1841.

─────────────────── ✧ ───────────────────

Exactly one month after he was sworn in as president, William Henry Harrison died, on April 4, 1841. It was the first time the United States lost its sitting president. No one knew exactly what would happen next.

The cabinet, the president's closest advisers, quickly sent word to Vice President Tyler, back home in Virginia. Tyler rushed to Washington in twenty-one hours by horseback and steamboat. As he traveled, Tyler thought about the Constitution. He arrived before sunrise on April 6, certain that he was president.

Mourners gather around Harrison's deathbed. His death in office was the first time that a vice president was called to Washington to replace a president.

✧ ————————

Others were not convinced. Former president John Quincy Adams wrote in his diary, "This is the first instance of a Vice-President being called to act as President of the United States, and brings to the test that provision of the Constitution which places in the Executive chair a man never thought of for it by an body."

CHAPTER THREE

WHO IS PRESIDENT?

*I am the President . . . when you think
otherwise, your resignations will be accepted.*
—John Tyler, to his cabinet, 1841

When John Tyler arrived in Washington on April 6, he quickly settled in at the Indian Queen Hotel. It was there that he held his first cabinet meeting. Before Tyler had reached the nation's capital, the cabinet officers had already decided what his title would be: "Vice President, acting as President." Tyler saw things differently. He believed once President Harrison died, the presidency was his.

At that initial meeting, the cabinet members described how President Harrison had run the meetings. Each person—whether president or cabinet officer—had one vote. The group decided matters democratically. Tyler listened to the cabinet, then politely made it clear he would do things his own way. "I am very glad to have in my cabinet able statesmen as you," Tyler said. "But I can never consent to

As a courtesy to the departing president and his family, the incoming president often stayed in a nearby Washington hotel at the beginning of the new term. Following that practice, Tyler stayed at the Indian Queen Hotel (above). He even held his first cabinet meeting there.

———————————— ✧ ————————————

be dictated to as to what I shall or shall not do. . . . I am the President . . . when you think otherwise, your resignations will be accepted."

No cabinet members resigned then, but the cabinet's leader, Secretary of State Daniel Webster, was able to persuade the new leader to do one thing. Webster thought Tyler needed to take the oath of office before he could officially consider himself president. Tyler disagreed, but to calm Webster, he took the oath. *The Congressional Directory* records the start of Tyler's presidency as April 6, when he was sworn in, rather than April 4, when Harrison died. Tyler would be the third U.S. president in less than five weeks. Martin Van Buren left office on March 3, 1841. William Henry Harrison held the presidency for just one month. By April 1841, John Tyler had become president.

The day after Tyler was sworn in as the nation's tenth commander in chief, President William Henry Harrison was buried. Three days after taking the oath, Tyler released a written inaugural speech that read in part, "By a deplored event I was unexpectedly elevated to the Presidency. For the first time in our history a person elected to the Vice Presidency of the United States has had devolved upon him the Presidential office." Tyler would also be the first president to serve without a vice president.

The tenth president soon settled into his new duties. By April 14, Tyler's wife Letitia and five of their nine children had moved from Williamsburg to Washington, D.C. Letitia had had a stroke in 1838 and was not able to perform the First Lady's traditional hostess duties. Instead, the Tylers' daughter-in-law Priscilla, who was married to their son Robert, stepped in as White House hostess.

Congress wasn't sure how to treat Tyler. On May 31, the House of Representatives debated whether Tyler was or was not the president. One Pennsylvania representative, John McKeon, introduced a resolution saying that Tyler should be considered an acting president until Congress decided how to choose a permanent new president. That resolution failed. Eventually, the representatives ended up passing a measure declaring that Tyler was indeed president. The Senate also debated the subject and also voted to recognize Tyler.

Tyler's confidence that he was the true president probably helped the country get through a difficult time. Since Tyler, eight vice presidents have become the country's top leader because of the death or resignation of the sitting president. Those vice presidents have followed what is known as the Tyler Precedent, the example that Tyler set. If the president dies or becomes unable to perform the job, the vice president assumes the presidency. And just as Tyler did, every vice president who steps into the commander in chief's job has also taken the oath of office.

James Madison
and the Constitution

If James Madison had lived a few more years, John Tyler's life might have turned out differently. But Madison, the country's fourth president and the last surviving member of the Constitutional Convention, died in 1836, five years before Tyler landed in the White House.

Madison is known as the Father of the Constitution, the document that spells out the basic laws of the United States. The Constitution didn't describe precisely what was supposed to happen when a president could no longer fulfill the job. But Madison's notes from the 1787 Constitutional Convention offer more details. The notes, which weren't published until long after Tyler was president, reveal that the men who wrote the Constitution believed that if a president died, his vice president would take over temporarily. The notes say that the vice president "shall exercise [the President's] powers and duties until another President be chosen."

Madison assumed that the country would call a special election to replace a president who died or was removed from office. But details about a presidential special election weren't included in the final draft of the Constitution. The final version reads: "In Case of the Removal of the President from Office or of his Death, Resignation, or Inability to discharge the Powers and Duties of the said Office, the Same shall devolve on [fall to] the Vice President."

When William Henry Harrison died in 1841, five years after Madison's death, no members of the Constitutional Convention were alive to offer guidance. Tyler read the Constitution one way. He assumed he was the rightful president. Others, including the country's sixth president, John Quincy Adams,

James Madison
——————— ✧

interpreted the Constitution differently. Adams and others like him never considered Tyler an official president. Chances are, James Madison wouldn't have considered John Tyler the true president either.

It took the country a long time to set into law just what should happen if a president needs to be replaced. The Twenty-fifth Amendment to the U.S. Constitution, which was passed in 1967, settled the issue. The amendment is clear, noting "In case of removal of the President from office or of his death or resignation, the Vice President shall become President."

During the Tyler administration, another presidential tradition got started that continues in modern times. The song "Hail to the Chief" began to be played as the presidential theme song.

For the first eight months of Tyler's presidency, the White House was open for socializing every evening.

"HAIL TO THE CHIEF"

The melody of the song now known as "Hail to the Chief" was adapted from an old Scottish tune for a theater production of Sir Walter Scott's poem, "The Lady of the Lake."

For a celebration of George Washington's birthday in 1815, the lyrics were rewritten:

Hail to the Chief we have chosen for the nation,
Hail to the Chief! We salute him, one and all.
Hail to the Chief, as we pledge cooperation
In proud fulfillment of a great, noble call.

Yours is the aim to make this grand country grander,
This you will do, That's our strong, firm belief.
Hail to the one we selected as commander,
Hail to the President! Hail to the Chief!

The U.S. Marine Band played the song at numerous public events attended by U.S. presidents in the early nineteenth century. It wasn't until Tyler's presidency that the band began to play it each time the president made an official appearance. By that time, the song had its modern title, "Hail to the Chief."

MISS COOPER AS HELENA.

*Priscilla Cooper had been an actress before
she married Tyler's son Robert.*

———————————— ◇ ————————————

Daughter-in-law Priscilla, who had made a name for herself as an actress, delivered an impressive performance
as the nation's premier hostess. She planned receptions,
dinners, and open houses. Cardboard prints of Priscilla
Tyler were popular items sold around the country. The
New York Sun wrote, "She has sound judgment . . . a keen
perception of the true and the false . . . without being
affected by false flattery. . . . She understands human
nature perfectly."

Priscilla Tyler knew how to make a good impression,
but in her private diary, she was not afraid to be blunt.

AN INNOCENT PARTY

The president's granddaughter, Mary Fairlee Tyler, daughter of Tyler's son Robert and his wife Priscilla, was the first child to have her birthday party at the White House. Before her marriage, Priscilla had performed in William Shakespeare's play, *A Midsummer Night's Dream*. The play had kept fairies popular in European culture—and eventually European American culture—since its first performance in the 1590s.

So three-year-old Mary attended her White House birthday party dressed as a wood fairy, complete with wings, crown, and wand. "There is more innocence in that room than ever there was before, or ever will be again—until we have another children's party," the White House doorkeeper said.

✧ ——————
Oberon and Titania, king and queen of the fairies in A Midsummer Night's Dream, *are shown here in an illustration from the late 1700s.*

Priscilla wrote that British author Charles Dickens wore "too much jewelry" and that the Russian foreign minister was "unusually hideous," while the British foreign minister was "a perfect bat." Priscilla relished her role as hostess, saying, "It is so easy to entertain, at other people's expense."

Normally, Congress gives the president money to cover the costs of maintaining the White House. But for much of Tyler's term, Congress refused to authorize any money to pay for White House expenses. Tyler himself had to pay for entertaining, heating, lighting, and keeping up the White House. Still, he remained polite. The *New York Herald* described the president's "natural courtesy, simple dignity, and the manner in which he puts his guests at ease."

A DAY IN THE LIFE OF THE PRESIDENT

Tyler's schedule was anything but easy. The president began his duties by sunrise, if not earlier, working by candlelight. He had breakfast at nine with his family, then went back to work. Here's how the president described his schedule: "First, all diplomatic matters; second, all matters connected with the action of Congress; third, matters of general concern falling under executive control; then the reception of visitors, and dispatch of private petitions [writing letters to grant citizens' requests for help from the president]."

After a midafternoon dinner and horseback ride, Tyler would meet with officials and citizens at White House gatherings until ten each evening. The busy schedule suited Tyler, who wrote, "So unceasing [endless] are my engagements that I rarely hear anything of the abuse of the [enemies] who are perpetually assailing [constantly attacking] me."

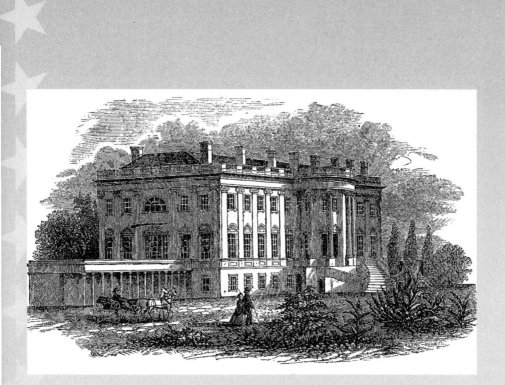

INSIDE THE WHITE HOUSE

When John Tyler was president, Washington, D.C., was still surrounded by swamps and only partly developed. The White House *(above)* was open to anyone who cared to visit.

Famous English novelist Charles Dickens visited the U.S. capital and strolled right into the White House. He "entered a large hall, and, having twice or thrice rung a bell which nobody answered, walked without further ceremony through the rooms on the ground floor, as [many] other gentlemen (mostly with their hats on, and their hands in their pockets), were doing very leisurely."

Dickens wandered up to the White House's second floor to meet with the president, but "no sentry guarded the door, no attendant stood behind the chief executive; no one asked the visitor to produce identification or even state his business." A messenger escorted Dickens into John Tyler's office, where "at a business-like table covered with papers, sat the President himself. He looked somewhat worn and anxious— and well he might: being at war with everybody,—but the expression of his face was mild and pleasant, and his manner remarkably unaffected, gentlemanly, and agreeable. I thought that, in his whole carriage and demeanor, he became his station singularly well."

The White House household budget wasn't much. Tyler, like every president back to George Washington, relied upon family members to perform jobs, sometimes without pay. Tyler's sons, John and Robert, both worked as White House presidential secretaries. Tyler's oldest son, Robert, also worked in the Land Office. Daughters Lizzy (Elizabeth) and Letty served as hostesses, alongside their sister-in-law Priscilla. It was only after a drunken man threw rocks at President Tyler, who was walking on the White House grounds, that Congress voted to create a security force of sixteen people to protect the White House.

Tyler faced relentless criticism as president of the United States.

✧ —————————

From the time he first took over the presidency, Tyler faced critics—some who believed he had no right to be the president and others who wanted to control his position. Senator Henry Clay of Tennessee, a leader of the Whig Party, certainly tried to control the White House. Clay wanted Tyler to know that he, as a leader of the party and a leader in the Senate, should be the boss, not the president. "If the Executive will cordially cooperate in carrying out the Whig measures, all will be well," Clay wrote. "Otherwise everything is at hazard."

The country was already facing tough economic times. A New York business leader noted that "business of no kind is healthy or prosperous." In February one of the United States' top banks, the United States Bank of Philadelphia, had failed. It didn't have enough money to cover withdrawals. To deal with the nation's money problems, William

Henry Harrison had called a special session of Congress, which was to convene in May 1841.

ECONOMIC AND POLITICAL TURMOIL

Just what would happen during the special session wasn't clear. What was certain were the deep divisions in the country. It didn't take the new president long to understand what he faced. "When I arrived here or within a day or two after, I became fully apprized [informed] of the angry

─────────────── ✦ ───────────────

Senator Henry Clay (standing center) *addresses the Senate.*
He was a powerful public speaker.

state of the factions [opposing groups] toward each other. . . . I was surrounded by Clay men, Webster men, AntiMormons, AntiMasons, original Harrisonians, old Whigs and new Whigs, each jealous of each other and all struggling for the offices," Tyler recalled.

The nation was growing and so was resentment among citizens and political parties. The 1840s saw the first major outbreak of nativism—discrimination against newcomers to the United States. Some members of Congress wanted to discourage immigrants from coming to the United States. These congressmen said that the country didn't have enough room or jobs for all those who wanted to come. The U.S. population had almost doubled in twenty years, from about 9.5 million people in 1820 to 17 million in 1840. One bill in Congress would have required newcomers to live in the United States for twenty-five years, instead of the standard five years, before they could become citizens.

President Tyler had to deal with all these issues. But the main problem was the country's struggling economy. The nation had never recovered from the hard economic times of 1837. Henry Clay and the Whigs wanted Tyler to reestablish a national bank. Clay believed that this bank would help the country control the money supply and prevent further economic depressions. But the Whigs hadn't been willing to put their national bank plan into their presidential platform. They never said during the 1840 presidential campaign that they intended to create a national bank. Tyler, still a Whig but against the bank, urged Clay and other congressional leaders not to bring up the bank plan during the upcoming special session.

AMERICAN CITIZENS!

We appeal to you in all calmness. Is it not time to pause ? Already the enemies of our dearest institutions, like the foreign spies in the Trojan horse of old, are within our gates. They are disgorging themselves upon us, at the rate of Hundreds or Thousands every year ! They aim at nothing short of conquest and supremacy over us.

A PAPER ENTITLED THE

AMERICAN PATRIOT.

CONSTITUTION AND LAWS

IN FAVOR OF	OPPOSED TO	
The protection of American Mechanics against Foreign Pauper Labor. Foreigners having a residence in the country of 21 years before voting. Our present Free School System. Carrying out the laws of the State, as regards sending back Foreign Paupers and Criminals.	Papal Aggression & Roman Catholicism. Foreigners holding office. Raising Foreign Military Companies in the United States. Nunneries and the Jesuits. To being taxed for the support of Foreign paupers millions of dollars yearly. To secret Foreign Orders in the U. S.	We are burdened with enormous taxes by foreigners. We are corrupted in the morals of our youth. We are interfered with in our government. We are forced into collisions with other nations. We are tampered with in our religion. We are injured in our labor. We are assailed in our freedom of speech.

The **PATRIOT** is Published by **J. E. Farwell & Co.**, **32 Congress St., Boston**, And for Sale at the Periodical Depots in this place. Single copies 4 Cents.

A mid-nineteenth-century announcement for a new newspaper expresses a common theme in U.S. nativist literature—discrimination against newcomers because of fear of foreign domination. Nativists feared that if too many Roman Catholic immigrants entered the country, the pope might try to interfere with the U.S. government.

✧

Tyler, who had long believed in states' rights, felt that a national bank could only exist if states had some control over it. He thought each state legislature should have the power to decide if the national bank could open a branch in that state. Clay and other Whigs thought a federal bank should have the authority to open branches wherever it felt necessary.

MESSAGE

FROM

THE PRESIDENT OF THE UNITED STATES,

RETURNING, WITH HIS OBJECTIONS, THE BILL TO

INCORPORATE THE FISCAL BANK OF THE UNITED STATES.

AUGUST 16, 1841.

To the Senate of the United States:

The bill entitled "An act to incorporate the subscribers to the Fiscal Bank of the United States," which originated in the Senate, has been considered by me, with a sincere desire to conform my action in regard to it to that of the two Houses of Congress. By the constitution it is made my duty either to approve the bill by signing it, or to return it, with my objections, to the House in which it originated. I cannot conscientiously give it my approval, and I proceed to discharge the duty required of me by the constitution—to give my reasons for disapproving.

The power of Congress to create a national bank to operate *per se* over the Union, has been a question of dispute from the origin of our Government. Men most justly and deservedly esteemed for their high intellectual endowments, their virtue, and their patriotism, have, in regard to it, entertained different and conflicting opinions. Congresses have differed. The approval of one President has been followed by the disapproval of another. The people, at different times, have acquiesced in decisions both for and against. The country has been, and still is, deeply agitated by this unsettled question. It will suffice for me to say, that my own opinion has been uniformly proclaimed to be against the exercise of any such power by this Government. On all suitable occasions, during a period of twenty-five years, the opinion thus entertained has been unreservedly expressed. I declared it in the Legislature of my native State. In the House of Representatives of the United States it has been openly vindicated by me. In the Senate Chamber, in the presence and hearing of many who are at this time members of that body, it has been affirmed and reaffirmed, in speeches and reports there made, and by votes there recorded. In popular assemblies I have unhesitatingly announced it; and in the last public declaration which I made, and that but a short time before the late presidential election, I referred to my previously-expressed opinions as being those then entertained by me. With a full knowledge of the opinions thus entertained, and never concealed, I was elected by the people Vice President of the United States. By the occurrence of a contingency provided for by the constitution, and arising under an impressive dispensation of Providence, I succeeded to the presidential office. Before entering upon the duties of that office, I took an oath that I would "preserve, protect, and defend the constitution of the United States." Entertaining the opinions alluded to, and having taken this oath, the Senate and the country will see that I could not give my sanction to a measure of the character described, without surrendering all claim to the respect of honorable men—all confidence on the part of the people—all self-respect—all regard for moral and religious obligations; without an observance of which no Government can be prosperous, and no people can be happy. It would be to commit a crime which I would not wilfully commit to gain any earthly reward, and which would justly subject me to the ridicule and scorn of all virtuous men

In this document addressed to the U.S. Senate, Tyler carefully presented his reasons against creating a national bank. Whig leader Senator Henry Clay was pushing a plan for a national bank.

✧ ——————————

By August, Congress had passed Clay's plan for the national bank. On August 16, Tyler vetoed the bank bill, setting the stage for a dramatic showdown with Clay, one of the nation's top orators (speakers) and the leader of the Whigs, the president's own political party.

On August 19, 1841, Henry Clay took center stage. Speaking in the Senate for more than an hour and a half, he lashed out against Tyler. Clay charged Tyler with being a vain and egotistical man who could not "see beyond the little, petty, contemptible circles of his own personal interests." Clay's bitter words hurt Tyler. But the hard feelings between the two men would soon become much worse.

*Tyler stood by his principles as president of the United States,
but his ideals cut him off from his political party.*

CHAPTER 4

PRESIDENT
WITHOUT A PARTY

*I pray you to believe that my back is to the
wall and that while I . . . deplore the assaults,
I shall . . . beat back the assailants [attackers].*

—John Tyler

Henry Clay and other Whigs were enraged by President
Tyler's veto of the national bank bill. It was a tense time
for U.S. leaders. Moderate Whigs like Secretary of State
Daniel Webster were torn. Their party was furious with
Tyler. But Tyler was the president, and Webster knew Tyler
had supported many important bills, from giving the navy
money for more ships to backing the Pre-Emption Act,
which offered settlers cheap land. Webster was so worried
about the tensions between Tyler and Clay that he couldn't
sleep at night.

When Tyler vetoed an amended bank bill on September
9, 1841, the Whigs erupted in anger. By September 11, five

of the six members of the president's cabinet had quit. Only Daniel Webster chose to stand by the embattled president. "Where am I to go, Mr. President?" Webster asked. Tyler left the decision up to Webster, saying, "You must decide that for yourself." Webster answered, "If you leave it to me, Mr. President, I will stay where I am." "Give me your hand on that," a delighted Tyler told Webster. "And now I say to you that Henry Clay is a doomed man."

Webster was working on a crucial treaty with Great Britain to settle the boundary between Maine and

Daniel Webster had been working on a border dispute about timber rights between Maine and the Canadian province of New Brunswick since early 1839. In this political cartoon, Britain's young Queen Victoria (left, seated on a dog) scolds U.S. president Van Buren (right, seated on an ox) for "threaten[ing] a young woman with a war about a few sticks of timber."

Canada and wanted to be sure it was done without interruption. He also disapproved of Clay's combative attitude toward the president. Webster wrote, "The truth is, the friends of Mr. Clay, some of them, seek to embarrass the President in all things." Webster knew the bitterness between Tyler and Clay could prevent the government from doing what was best for the country. He saw that the president resented Clay's aggressive attitude, noting "between their factious [quarrelsome] spirits & [Tyler's] resentment of what he regards as intended insult no one can tell what may happen to the public interest."

Tyler believed he had to rush to fill the five empty cabinet posts. The resignations took effect on Saturday, September 11, during the special session of Congress that was scheduled to end two days later. Tyler and others thought that any resignations that occurred during a special session had to be filled during that same session. So Tyler scurried to find replacements for five key cabinet jobs over the weekend. By September 13, Monday morning, he had a list of names. They included two northerners and three southerners, all Democratic lawyers who had become Whigs. Congress approved the president's new cabinet choices and then adjourned (ended the session).

THE WHIGS VS. TYLER

Whig members of Congress weren't done expressing their outrage at Tyler. The same day the special session adjourned, about five dozen Whig members of Congress met in a Washington, D.C., public square. They voted

U.S. representative John Minor Botts of Virginia

to accept a proclamation explaining their opposition to Tyler's bank veto. Representative John Minor Botts of Virginia, Tyler's home state, accused the president of treachery. "It is impossible to serve God and Mammon [money] both. So I conceived it impossible to serve Mr. Tyler and my country at the same time," Botts claimed.

Not all Whigs agreed that Tyler deserved to be punished. Representative George Proffit of Indiana stood up to defend the president. He said, "From the first meeting of Congress up to this hour, there has been a determination on the part of some gentlemen to create an issue with the

President . . . to make him sign a bill which neither his conscience nor his judgment approved." Two Whig representatives ended up hitting one another and nearly fought a duel.

It wasn't just Tyler's veto of a national bank that angered Whigs. Clay and others deeply resented Tyler for not letting them control how the White House voted on the issues. The Whigs wanted government limits on presidential vetoes and increased congressional power. Tyler, who had made a career of standing up for states' rights rather than the rights of a strong federal government, sat in the White House, defending the power of the president.

The Whigs felt betrayed. They voted to expel Tyler, the president of the United States, from the Whig Party. They printed twenty thousand copies of their manifesto—their charges against Tyler—and circulated the copies nationwide.

Within days, anger against the stubborn president spread around the country. Whigs in a dozen cities began burning effigies, crude figures that were supposed to represent the president. The Whigs paid troublemakers to protest against Tyler. Most Americans weren't that concerned about a national bank, let alone Whig Party politics. Still, President Tyler couldn't ignore the Whigs' hostility. The White House received hundreds of death threat letters, while newspapers printed countless angry editorials.

Tyler refused to yield. "From the moment of my assuming the helm . . . my ship [was] tempest-tossed," he wrote. Tyler saw himself as the captain of a ship in a storm. As a vice president who took over when a president died, he felt alone and without support from the former president's political party.

MUTINY!

Not every political problem President Tyler faced centered on the Whigs. Tyler also had to resolve a sticky situation involving a mutiny.

It started when Secretary of War John C. Spencer's son, Philip, was serving on board the *Somers*, a training ship for potential naval officers. Nineteen-year-old Philip Spencer and others planned to kill the ship's officer so they could take control of the *Somers* and use it to attack merchant (trading) ships and plunder their riches. The ship's master commander, Alexander Slidell Mackenzie, found out about the plot and had Spencer and two other would-be pirates executed.

War secretary Spencer wanted Mackenzie tried for murder in a civilian (nonmilitary) court for killing Philip. Navy secretary Abel Upshur chose to have Mackenzie court-martialed (face a military trial) instead. When the verdict was announced that Mackenzie was to be acquitted (found innocent), the war secretary was outraged. He wanted the president to order a

John C. Spencer

new trial. But the navy secretary recommended that Tyler let the acquittal stand. The two cabinet officers—Spencer and Upshur—quarreled, and the president tried to find a compromise. Tyler let Mackenzie's acquittal stand, but the naval officer was never assigned to another ship.

Even moderate Daniel Webster drew fire for staying with the president. Someone described the secretary of state as looking "black as a thundercloud, and careworn." Despite the Whigs' pressure tactics, Webster, like Tyler, stood firm, saying, "We shall stand steady here, let the storm beat ever so hard."

Economic and political matters in Washington weren't the only storms pounding the White House. In the fall of 1841, slaves revolted on board the *Creole,* a U.S. ship sailing from Virginia to New Orleans, Louisiana. The slaves mutinied, took over the ship, and landed in the Bahamas, a group of Caribbean islands controlled by Great Britain. Britain had outlawed slavery, so the British officials freed the slaves who hadn't been involved in the mutiny. The outraged American owners of the slaves demanded to be reimbursed for the cost of their lost human property. The United States and Britain argued over the matter for years.

Tyler knew he couldn't spend years solving the country's economic woes. He had to do something fast to fix the money supply. He and his new cabinet began working on what they called the Exchequer Plan. Tyler envisioned a government institution controlled by the U.S. treasurer, the treasury secretary, and three other board members appointed by the president to oversee and control the nation's money supply. Under Tyler's plan, Congress would have power to modify or shut down the Exchequer. But when Congress met again in December 1841, Clay and other Whigs ignored Tyler's plan.

The president had few allies and many enemies. After less than a year as president, Tyler could count on the loyalty of just one senator and two members of the House of Representatives. His fellow Virginians criticized Tyler's abilities. John Strode Barbour said, "His ambition has warped a candid [truthful] mind." Benjamin Leigh complained of Tyler's "unscrupulousness [lack of morals], the folly [foolishness] and knavery [wickedness] of his ambition."

New Year's 1842 brought some brightness to the unpopular president. On January 31, 1842, Tyler's daughter Elizabeth was married at the White House. It would be the only time the First Lady Letitia Tyler would make a public appearance. Letitia's poor health kept her upstairs in a wheelchair, but she came down to see Lizzie marry William Waller. Lizzie and William's ceremony was only the second time a president's daughter was married at the White House. Her wedding would be the first of the Tyler family's milestones that year.

The new year brought a milestone in Congress as well. On February 23, 1842, Senator Henry Clay announced he was resigning from the Senate. Clay planned to run for president against Tyler, his fellow Whig. Whigs continued to be furious that Tyler refused to do what they wanted. Their anger grew hotter after Tyler wrote to a supporter that the Whigs expected him to be "a follower of a party; as he is required either to be a piece of wax to be molded in any shape others may please." Tyler wrote a Philadelphia supporter that "each branch of the government is independent of every other, and heaven forbid that day should ever come when either can dictate to the other. The Constitution never designed that the executive should be a mere cipher [person without worth or influence]."

President Tyler continued to battle Congress over how to replenish the U.S. Treasury, which was almost out of money. Tyler and Congress agreed that the government needed to raise tariffs, the taxes paid by foreign countries

In this detail from a political cartoon, "Old Veto" Tyler holds up his veto sword.

——————— ✧

exporting their goods to America. Over the summer, Congress passed two bills to raise tariffs, but Tyler vetoed them both, earning the nickname, "Old Veto."

The tariff bills Tyler refused to sign also included a plan to allow states to receive the money from the sale of federal lands. But Tyler wanted the federal government to receive the money from the public land sales. Tyler finally signed a tariff bill in late August, when Congress sent him a plan that didn't include anything about selling public land.

INTERNATIONAL PROGRESS

While Tyler wrestled with domestic issues, Secretary of State Daniel Webster was making progress on the international front. Webster negotiated a settlement with Lord Ashburton over a long-simmering border dispute with Great Britain. In August 1842, the United States and

Britain agreed on the border between Maine and Canada. The United States received a little more than half of the twelve thousand square miles—stretching east from the Great Lakes to the Atlantic Ocean—that the two countries had been squabbling about. The Webster-Ashburton pact, officially known as the Treaty of Washington, also outlined how the United States and Britain could cooperate to prevent slave trading, illegal in both countries, along the African coast.

The treaty pleased both Tyler and Webster. The secretary of state wrote the president that the treaty with Great Britain wouldn't have happened without Tyler's "anxious and intelligent attention to what was in progress." Tyler responded that the treaty provided "a set-off to the torrents of abuse. . . lavished upon me."

The Senate passed the treaty by a vote of 39 to 9, with only one Whig voting no. The Whigs held a celebration dinner in New York to honor Lord Ashburton before he went back to Great Britain but chose not to invite President Tyler. When the British diplomat stood to toast the absent president, the Whigs remained seated. Thousands of Americans were outraged at what they considered the Whigs' rude treatment of their leader. New Yorkers unfurled banners that read, "An Insult to the President Is An Insult to the Nation."

The president was also dealing with serious personal matters. "Your mother's health is bad," Tyler wrote his daughter Mary in July. "Her mind is greatly prostrated [overcome] by her disease and she seems quite anxious to have you with her."On September 10, 1842, First Lady Letitia Tyler died after suffering a second stroke. John Tyler was the first president to become a widower while in the White House.

Within a few months of Letitia's death, President Tyler had met another woman. Julia Gardiner was thirty years younger than the president. Her father, David, was a U.S. senator from New York. Julia met the president at a White House reception. Soon Tyler asked the young woman to marry him. Years later, Julia recalled the president's proposal, saying, "I had never thought of love, so I said, 'No, no, no,' and shook my head with each word, which flung the tassel of my Greek cap into his face with every move. It was undignified, but it amused me very much to see his expression." Still, the stubborn president pursued his young love.

———— ✧

Julia Gardiner modelled for this advertisement for Bogert & Mecambly, a department store probably located in New York City.

Fort Vancouver was founded in 1825 as a trading post on the Columbia River. The fort encouraged white settlers to come to Oregon Territory.

— ✧ —

Tyler and Secretary of State Daniel Webster continued to look ahead. The United States was stretching its boundaries, but its borders didn't include the West Coast. Oregon Territory was up for grabs. The area Tyler and his contemporaries called Oregon includes present-day Oregon, Washington, Idaho, and parts of Canada's British Columbia. Russia controlled the territory north of that, and Spain owned California. Those countries, along with the United States and Britain, were all vying for control of the Oregon Territory. Britons and Americans had occupied parts of the territory, but no country had staked a formal claim.

The elections in November 1842 pushed the Whigs out of power in the House of Representatives. The Whigs went from having 133 members of the House to just 79. Webster blamed the Whigs' defeat on the "violence and injustice which characterized the conduct of the Whig leaders." He feared the Whig Party was "broken up and perhaps never to be united." Tyler saw the Democrats' victory over the Whigs as a victory for himself as well. The president hoped that voters were tired of the Whigs' harsh stands. Tyler decided to build a new coalition of supporters that would include former Whigs and conservative Democrats.

In December 1842, Tyler sent a special message to Congress recognizing Hawaii's status as an independent nation. Although the Hawaiian Islands are thousands of

——————— ✧ ———————

Kamehameha III, king of Hawaii (left, in Westernized clothing), was a young man of twenty-eight when Tyler formally accepted the island nation's independence in a message to Congress.

miles from the coast of North America, Great Britain and France seemed interested in their rich resources. Tyler decided that the Monroe Doctrine extended to Hawaii. The doctrine, which dated to the 1820s when James Monroe was president, stated that Europe didn't have the right to colonize (settle) any land in the Western Hemisphere.

By late 1842, Tyler was looking ahead to the next presidential election. He began to try to ensure that people in government jobs would vote for him in the next election. "We have numberless enemies in office and they should forthwith be made to quit," Tyler said. The president told his treasury secretary to pay close attention when selecting U.S. marshals and attorneys. "We must be cautious and never appoint any other than a well known friend," Tyler said.

In December 1842, Tyler cast his fifth veto, refusing to sign another public land sale bill. Tyler's veto angered even southern Whigs, including those in his home state of Virginia.

IMPEACHMENT

In January 1843, Congress attempted once again to attack President Tyler. This time, instead of just kicking him out of the Whig Party or overturning his vetoes, Congress did something it had never tried to do before. It tried to impeach, or force out, the president. The Constitution says that a president "shall be removed from office on impeachment for, and conviction of, treason, bribery, or other high crimes and misdemeanors." John Minor Botts, the representative from Tyler's home state of Virginia, led the impeachment drive. He claimed that Tyler had committed a crime by abusing his power.

It's Not Easy to Impeach a President

Only the House of Representatives can vote to impeach a president. Impeachment means to charge a president or other top government official with wrongdoing. If the House votes for impeachment, the Senate holds a trial. At the Senate trial, the chief justice of the Supreme Court acts as the judge and the Senate acts as the jury. If two-thirds of the senators find the president guilty of impeachment charges, he is convicted and is legally no longer president.

The impeachment resolution outraged Tyler, who replied, "I have been accused without evidence and condemned without a hearing. . . . I am charged with violating pledges which I never gave [and]. . . with usurping [taking] powers not conferred upon [given to] the President by law."

Tyler wanted his response to the impeachment charges to be included in the *Congressional Record,* the official written record of the meetings of the U.S. Senate and House of Representatives, but they weren't. The president didn't have the power to control Congress. Still, by a vote of 127 to 83, the House rejected the impeachment resolution. Tyler would remain in the White House, but he continued to be under attack from Whigs.

CHAPTER FIVE

GRIEF AND JOY

It is incredible that a jolly military song should
have delivered this man [Tyler] from
crippling injury or sudden death.

—James G. Birney, the antislavery Liberty Party's
U.S. presidential candidate in 1844

By March 1843, President Tyler was looking for new cabinet members again. War secretary John C. Spencer and treasury secretary Walter Forward resigned. Then Congress rejected Tyler's choice for treasury secretary, so Spencer agreed to take that post. The government seemed stalled by the endless friction between the White House and the Whig-led Senate. That month navy secretary Abel Upshur wrote a friend, "I have no hope for the country."

But the greatest professional loss for the president occurred on May 8, when Secretary of State Daniel Webster resigned. Webster had stayed at his post to guide the treaty talks with Great Britain. Once they were done and work was under way on diplomatic talks about trade with China, Webster stepped down. Still, each man continued to respect the other. Tyler told Webster, "You have manifested [shown] powers of intellect of the highest order, and in all things [are] a true American."

Before Webster left office, the cabinet lost another member. On June 20, 1843, Attorney General Hugh Legaré died. Tyler shifted Navy secretary Upshur to Webster's spot and found another attorney general and navy secretary. In less than four years in office, President Tyler went through four secretaries of state, four treasury secretaries, five navy secretaries, four war secretaries, three attorneys general, and two postmasters general. His six-member cabinet would be the most disrupted one in U.S. history.

DEADLY ACCIDENT

On February 28, 1844, President Tyler and several cabinet members were on board the USS *Princeton,* a steamship. About 350 Washington, D.C., dignitaries had boarded the ship, anchored in the Potomac River, to see a demonstration of a new cannon called the Peacemaker. This wrought iron cannon had been designed by the ship's captain, Robert Stockton. Until the Peacemaker, cannons had been made of cast iron. Wrought iron is commercially purified and more workable than cast iron. Stockton said his new design was "substantially more powerful than any other in the world."

Stockton had successfully fired the Peacemaker twice and was preparing to fire the cannon once more for spectators. The president was below deck, his foot on the ladder to head upstairs to view the cannon blast again. Just then, Tyler's son-in-law, William Waller, who was below deck with

Abel Upshur

———— ✧ ————

the president, began singing a military song, so Tyler stepped down from the ladder to listen to Waller perform.

On the deck above, a roar erupted, and the Peacemaker cannon exploded. "Surgeons! All surgeons! To the deck at once!" screamed an officer, his face blackened with gunpowder. The cannon's malfunction slammed molten metal chunks around the deck, killing eight men, including the new secretary of state Abel Upshur and Navy secretary Thomas Gilmer, who had been in the job for just nine days. The accident also killed Senator David Gardiner, the father of the woman Tyler wanted to marry.

PRESIDENTIAL SLAVE OWNERS

John Tyler's body slave, who usually stayed by the president to attend to his personal needs, was among those killed when the Peacemaker cannon exploded on board the *Princeton* in February 1844. John Tyler continued to own slaves while he lived in the White House.

Eight other presidents—George Washington, Thomas Jefferson, James Madison, James Monroe, Andrew Jackson, James Polk, Zachary Taylor, and Andrew Johnson—also owned slaves. Ulysses Grant was given one slave but quickly freed the man.

The Peacemaker cannon explosion was a tragic accident
that changed Tyler's life in many ways.

——————————— ✧ ———————————

The explosion stunned the public. Many expressed amazement that President Tyler had escaped injury, through simple chance. "It is incredible that a jolly military song should have delivered this man from crippling injury or death," noted one bystander.

The fatal accident aboard the *Princeton* spared the president and also gave him another chance with Julia Gardiner. "After I lost my father," she said, "I felt differently toward the President. He seemed to fill the place and to be more agreeable in every way than any younger man ever was or could be."

Julia's mother, Julianna, was a powerful New York society woman. She wasn't convinced the president was good enough for her daughter. Tyler wrote Julianna asking permission to marry Julia. He reminded Julianna about his "position in Society" as president. Julianna asked if he would be able to provide the "necessary comforts and elegancies of life" for Julia. Tyler didn't have as much money as the Gardiners, but he wasn't poor. Eventually, Julianna was persuaded that the president would make a good son-in-law.

ANNEXING TEXAS

President Tyler wanted to do something that would make his presidency memorable. He thought that if he could help Texas become part of the United States, he would earn his place in history books. His new secretary of state, John C. Calhoun of South Carolina, also backed the Texas plan. So in April 1844, Tyler asked Congress to approve a treaty with Texas that would allow the United States to annex (take possession of) the independent territory of Texas.

Adding Texas to the United States was complicated. Northern states were concerned that Texas would be broken up into as many as five states, each of which would allow slavery. That would tip the political balance so that Congress would have more members from slave states than from free states. Southern states wanted Texas to join the United States to give them greater power in Congress.

On June 8, after three weeks of debate, Congress rejected Tyler's plan to annex Texas. Henry Clay was delighted that "Mr. Tyler's abominable treaty" wasn't approved. Two days after Congress rejected annexation, Tyler asked it to grant Texas statehood as just one state. Congress still refused.

A Lone Star

Americans had been living in the Mexican territory of Texas for years. Mexico had encouraged Americans to cross the border and colonize Texas, as long as they were not slave owners and became Catholic, Mexico's national religion. But the Americans who went to Texas broke both agreements. By the late 1830s, about twenty thousand Americans had moved to Texas. They ignored Mexico's wishes, and eventually, Mexico sent soldiers to control the unruly settlers. Mexico and Americans living in Texas continued to fight over who would control the territory.

In February 1836, the Mexican army, led by General Santa Anna, surrounded the Alamo, a chapel that had been turned into a fortress. About 180 Texans, including Davy Crockett and James Bowie, were inside the Alamo. They refused to surrender to the thousands of Mexican soldiers. On March 6, after a two-week siege, hand-to-hand combat broke out. All the Alamo's defenders died.

⸻ ✧ ⸻

Texans fought Mexico's army in the famous battle of the Alamo in 1836.

Texas then declared itself independent. Mexico was not eager to give up the vast territory. Santa Anna's army continued to fight Texans. At the Battle of San Jacinto in April 1836, Texas commander Sam Houston surprised the Mexican army and managed to capture Santa Anna. After that, Mexico withdrew its soldiers south of the river known as the Rio Grande. Still Mexico refused to acknowledge that Texas was independent, though Texans considered themselves free. By the end of the year, Houston was elected president of the independent Republic of Texas.

In March 1837, one year and one day after Texas declared its independence, President Andrew Jackson issued a presidential proclamation recognizing Texas's independence from Mexico. Jackson signed the proclamation on his last day as president.

Tyler followed Jackson's example. As Tyler's time in the White House drew to a close, he too would use his last hours in office to take a strong stand on Texas.

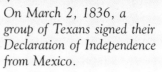

On March 2, 1836, a group of Texans signed their Declaration of Independence from Mexico.

Julia Gardiner Tyler

THE PRESIDENT ELOPES

On June 26, 1844, four months after her father died and close to two years after First Lady Letitia Tyler died, the president and Julia Gardiner were secretly married in New York. The wedding was so secret that not even all of Tyler's children knew it was happening. His son John Jr. was the president's best man, but Tyler chose not to tell his four daughters about the marriage until afterward. Lizzie, Mary, Alice, and Letty were hurt that their father didn't confide in them. Letty never accepted Julia as her stepmother. Julia was five years younger than Mary, Tyler's oldest child, and just ten years older than Tazewell, his youngest.

Tyler's daughters weren't the only ones taken by surprise when fifty-four-year-old John and twenty-four-year-old Julia eloped. People around the country were stunned. The *New York Herald*'s joking headline read, "Treaty of Immediate Annexation; Ratified Without the Consent of the Senate." Tyler wrote his daughter Mary that Julia "is all I could wish her to be. . . the most beautiful woman of the age and at the same time the most accomplished."

Not everyone approved of the match. Former president John Quincy Adams wrote in his diary that the newlyweds were "the laughingstock of Washington, D.C." Another politician, Philip Howe, called Tyler "the old fool." Tyler, the first vice president to succeed a president, set another first. He became the first president to be married while in office. The newlywed Tylers were the first presidential couple to be photographed in the White House.

As president, Tyler couldn't escape from his job for a lengthy honeymoon. Within days, he and Julia were back in Washington, where they held a White House reception. Soon, though, the couple found ways to get away from the nation's capital. They spent time during the summer of 1844 staying at a government-owned cottage at Fortress Monroe, Virginia. The fort's commander had ordered his staff to fix up the four-room cottage for

The Tylers slipped away to a cottage at Fortress Monroe, Virginia, for a few vacation days in 1844. The fort protected a busy Atlantic Ocean port.

————————————— ✧ —————————————

the newlyweds. Julia preferred the War Department bungalow to the White House. She wrote, "True love in a cottage, and quite a contrast to my dirty establishment in Washington. It seemed quite as if I had stepped into paradise."

Julia was probably not exaggerating about the grungy conditions at the White House. To spite Tyler, Congress still refused to appropriate (set aside) money for basic White House upkeep and repairs. Tyler continued to pay for this out of his own pocket on a salary of $25,000 a year. Tyler's new mother-in-law paid to clean and decorate the White House. "You know how I detest a dirty house," Julianna wrote her daughter.

A MOTHER'S ADVICE

The First Lady's mother, Julianna Gardiner, was never afraid to offer advice. When she learned that Julia was going into Tyler's office during the day and was seen kissing him in public, Julianna stepped in with some wise words: "Let your husband work during business hours," she lectured Julia. "Business should take the precedence of caressing—reserve your caressing for private leisure and be sure [to] let no one see it unless you wish to be laughed at."

Some of Julianna's no-nonsense advice about living life in the public eye at the White House still rings true. She told her daughter, "You must not mind any objections made of you in the newspapers. You will not escape censure [criticism]. Do your best."

Julianna was right that her daughter would not escape criticism. Although born and reared in New York, Julia was a strong supporter of slavery. Julia put herself into the middle of the national controversy over slavery when a British duchess appealed to southern women to oppose slavery. Julia retorted that the slave "lives sumptuously" compared to British industrial workers and that southerners had the right to decide upon their own institutions.

✧ ──────────

Julia Tyler's support for slavery was well known. This song, dedicated to her, mocks the American antislavery author Harriet Beecher Stowe.

Julia's mother wasn't the only Gardiner to become a frequent visitor at the White House. Julia's sister Margaret volunteered to act as the new First Lady's social secretary. Julia's young cousins became her attendants. Together, they would sit on couches that were on a dais, a raised platform. Some people criticized the young bride for acting like a queen. But what sparked the most attention were the dances Julia hosted. While married to Letitia, Tyler had disapproved of dancing. He wrote his daughter Mary that one popular dance, the waltz, was "rather vulgar" and that he would prefer she avoid waltzing. But Julia persuaded the president that dancing was a fine entertainment. Soon White House balls opened with waltzes. Even after he retired from the White House, Tyler still received angry letters from ministers about Julia's dances.

As President Tyler's term drew closer to an end, he continued to try to make progress on matters at home and abroad. Even without Daniel Webster, Tyler's administration succeeded in accomplishing major diplomatic goals. The United States was hungry to build ties in the Far East

——————————— ✧
Congressman Caleb Cushing of Massachusetts represented the United States in the treaty negotiations with China.

British soldiers watch British officers shake hands with Chinese officials when Hong Kong is transferred to British control in 1842.

with China. In 1842 China and Great Britain had signed a treaty that gave the island of Hong Kong to the British and opened trade with China, the world's largest country. Tyler wanted the United States to be able to trade with China as well. In 1844 the United States and China signed the Treaty of Wanghia, which regulated trade between the two countries.

The Treaty of Wanghia, the first U.S. treaty with China, was signed on July 3, 1844, in this Buddhist temple on the former Portuguese island of Macao. (The island has been part of China since 1999.)

✧

Tyler had also negotiated a treaty with the Zollverein, a group of twenty German states. But the Senate rejected that treaty, saying that the president didn't have the power to control foreign policy. The Senate Foreign Relations Committee told Tyler that the president's job was "to follow, not to lead, and to fulfill, not to ordain [create] the law."

Tyler played an important role in Texas's transition from independence to statehood. The flag of the independent Republic of Texas, adopted in 1839, became the state flag of Texas in 1845.

CHAPTER SIX

POLITICS, TEXAS STYLE

*If the annexation of Texas shall crown off my
public life, I shall neither retire ingloriously
[without honor] nor soon be forgotten.*

—John Tyler

John Tyler wanted to be reelected in 1844. But he did
not have much of a chance. The Whig Party had already
disowned him. Henry Clay, Tyler's longtime political
enemy, was running for president on the Whig ticket. The
Democrats weren't going to nominate Tyler, a former Whig.
But the president did have enough power to help influence
which candidate the Democrats would choose. Tyler's strat-
egy centered on Texas. He wanted the Lone Star Republic
to become part of the United States. Tyler did everything
he could to make sure that Texas was a key issue in the
1844 election. Henry Clay and the Whigs opposed annexation, but many southern Democrats wanted Texas for the
United States.

The Whigs did not support Tyler for reelection in 1844. The Whig candidates that year were Henry Clay (top) for president and Theodore Frelinghuysen (bottom) for vice president.

✧ ——————————

To strengthen his bid to annex Texas, Tyler even launched his own political party, the John Tyler Party. This time, the campaign slogan was "Tyler and Texas." Tyler chose to hold his new party's convention in Baltimore, at the same time the Democrats were meeting to choose their presidential candidate. The Democrats refused to endorse former president Martin Van Buren because he opposed Texas annexation. Democratic leaders worried that if they chose Van Buren, some Democrats would leave the party and vote for Tyler instead. To prevent that, the Democrats nominated James Polk, who favored expanding the United States to include both Texas and Oregon.

The John Tyler Party planned to back candidates in every national race in New York, New Jersey, and Pennsylvania. Democrats feared Tyler supporters would drain votes from Polk and indirectly help the Whigs' candidate Clay become president. Tyler didn't want Clay in the White House. So he made a deal with the Democrats.

Tyler had hoped former Democratic president Andrew Jackson would write a public letter praising him and welcoming Tyler's supporters back into the Democratic Party as "brethren and equals." Jackson refused, but the party did encourage some newspaper publishers to stop blasting the president.

The Democratic candidates for president, James K. Polk (left), and vice president, George M. Dallas (right), hoped to get some Whig votes in 1844. Like Tyler, they supported annexing Texas.

On August 20, 1844, the *Madisonian* newspaper printed a letter from Tyler titled "To My Friends throughout the Union." In the letter, Tyler asked Americans to consider whether the country was better off than it had been when he took office. By late in Tyler's presidency, the U.S. budget was balanced. But three years of political wrangling between Tyler and Whigs had limited what the president could accomplish.

Two days after his public letter, Tyler saw that he didn't have a chance to be reelected and withdrew his name from the race. But the president was not ready to give up his dream of making Texas part of the United States. He thought that Texas's massive size and key location would greatly enhance the nation. Tyler said the combination of the cotton grown in Texas with that grown in the rest of the South would mean the United States would have almost complete control of the cotton market. For years the president had wanted to annex the Lone Star State. Adding Texas to the United States would help raise his reputation as a statesman.

In October 1844, Tyler wrote Daniel Webster about annexing Texas, saying, "Could anything throw so bright a luster on us?" But many Democrats and Whigs saw Tyler's plans to annex Texas as proof of his loyalty to the South rather than to the United States as a whole. People thought Tyler wanted Texas to make the South stronger and keep slavery alive.

From his deathbed, former president Andrew Jackson wrote letters encouraging the annexation of Texas. According to Jackson, if the United States didn't annex Texas, the Lone Star State would find another protector—

Mourners gather around Andrew Jackson's deathbed.

likely Great Britain, which would demand that Texas be a free state (where slavery was illegal). A British-controlled Texas could hurt the power of the United States and limit the southern states' power in Congress. Even though Tyler was a slave owner, he said he didn't care much about whether Texas would be a slave state or not. In his final year in office, Tyler pushed to make his Texas dream come true. In November voters elected Democrat James Polk to be the eleventh president, but Tyler still had a few months left in office—and he hadn't given up on Texas.

In December 1844, President Tyler once again asked Congress to pass a resolution making Texas a state. This time, Congress responded. The election of Polk, who favored expansion, made the annexation of Texas seem inevitable. The Senate passed a resolution to annex Texas on February 27, 1845. The House approved the same resolution the next day. The bill also stated that new states north of the southern boundary of Missouri would be free states but that Texas, which could be cut into up to five separate states, could allow slavery. Tyler signed the joint resolution on March 1, just three days before his presidential term ended.

Also in February, the president and First Lady hosted a White House gala. One thousand candles shone in the East Room. Waiters served nearly one hundred bottles of champagne. About two thousand people were invited to say good-bye to the president. Tyler, ever gallant, joked about his sudden popularity, saying, "They cannot say now that I am a *President without a party.*"

The president who led the country without the support of a political party had managed a number of achievements. His administration negotiated treaties with Britain, China, and Germany. By the time Texas officially became the twenty-eighth state, James Polk was in the White House. Still, Tyler had done the work to bring Texas into the Union. It could be said that Tyler lost the presidency but won Texas. A modern historian wrote that President Tyler's pattern was to manage "diplomatic triumph combined with personal political defeat."

CHAPTER SEVEN

VIRGINIA, PEACE, AND WAR

*I have been so rudely buffeted [hit] by the
waves of party politics, that I sigh for the quiet
of my country residence, and look most
anxiously to the . . . [time] when my connection
with political life will expire.*

—John Tyler

In March 1845, John Tyler left the White House. Much
had happened to him in the four years since he had been
elected vice president. For the first time, the United States
had lost its president, William Henry Harrison. Tyler had
assumed the presidency and quickly lost the support of his
party, the Whigs, who continued to oppose him throughout
his term in office. During those years, Tyler faced serious
domestic and international matters, from a depressed economy to trade and border conflicts with Britain, China, and
Mexico. Also during his presidential term, Tyler suffered the
death of his invalid wife, Letitia. And in another White

House first, he married Julia Gardiner, making him the first president to wed while in office.

John and Julia Tyler left Washington, D.C., and retired to a 1,150-acre estate near Richmond, Virginia. The home sat amid a grove of stately trees. Tyler named the estate Sherwood Forest, saying he felt like Robin Hood hiding out in the forest after being thrown out by the Whigs. Sherwood Forest was just three miles from his childhood home of Greenway. Once again, John Tyler was back in Charles City County. He assumed the life of the gentleman farmer, raising wheat and corn on his plantation. In July 1846, Julia gave birth to their son David. It was her first child and Tyler's tenth. As the years passed, their family continued to grow. Over the next fourteen years, Tyler's name would be mentioned again and again as a possible candidate for the presidency.

In modern times, John Tyler's heirs still own and live at Sherwood Forest.

ALL THE PRESIDENT'S CHILDREN

Fourteen of John Tyler's children—seven girls and seven boys—lived to adulthood. Their stories offer a glimpse of American history. The president's third child with Letitia, a son named John, served as an assistant secretary of War for the Confederacy, the government set up by the Southern states at the start of the Civil War (1861–1865). John's older brother, Robert, was register of the Confederate Treasury. David Gardiner Tyler *(right)*, the president's first child with Julia, was a member of the U.S. House of Representatives and later a judge. Another of the president's children, Lyon Gardiner Tyler, was president of William and Mary College. Two other sons were doctors. Two daughters married farmers. Daughter Letty married a man who

David Gardiner Tyler

◇

served as paymaster (an officer who has the duty of handing out pay) in both the U.S. and later the Confederate navies. The president's last child, Pearl, was born when John Tyler was seventy years old. This was in 1860, just before the Civil War began. She died in 1947, just after World War II (1939–1945) ended.

*Tyler used this small building on his Sherwood Forest estate as a
law office. He had trouble earning enough money
as a lawyer to support his big family.*

———————————— ✧ ————————————

ROAD OVERSEER

Life at Sherwood Forest wasn't always easy. In 1850 Tyler
was so pressed for money that he couldn't pay a bill
for $1.25 until he sold his corn crop. Neighbors appointed
him to serve as overseer for maintaining the road leading
to Sherwood Forest. Although some might consider
it an insult to ask a former U.S. president to oversee
a road, Tyler chose to see it in a different way. He
said he was reminded of one of his favorite heroes,
Epaminondas, who was a warrior and statesman in ancient
Thebes, in Egypt. After winning Thebes's highest honors,
Epaminondas fell from favor. His enemies elected him a

*Tyler's role model,
Epaminondas, lived from
about 418–362* B.C.
──────── ✧

E PAMINONDAS .

public trash collector. As Tyler recalled, Epaminondas said if the "office could not reflect honor on him, he could reflect honor on the office." Later, when his neighbors decided Tyler was making them work too hard in maintaining the road, especially during their harvest times, they urged him to resign. But Tyler chose to keep his road job, saying, "Offices were hard to obtain in these times, and having no assurance that he would ever get another, he could not think, under the circumstances, of resigning."

Tyler, ever true to his beliefs, stayed steady, overseeing his road, his estate, his quiet country life. Gradually, Tyler's neighbors and other Whigs would come to appreciate the former president whom they had once sought to impeach.

On Tyler's sixty-second birthday, Julia wrote him a poem:

Then, listen, dearest, to my strain
and never doubt its truth
Thy ripen'd charms are all to me,
Wit I prefer to youth!

Julia and John had seven children together. No other president fathered as many children as Tyler—sixteen in all.

Despite the pain from his bruising presidency, Tyler continued to seek public roles. He was on the board of visitors of the College of William and Mary for more than three decades. In 1859 the college named Tyler to its highest post, chancellor. The last person to hold that office had been George Washington. Tyler called it "an honor of which I am quite as proud as any other ever conferred upon me by my fellowmen."

In 1860 Tyler spoke at a banquet honoring a Richmond monument to Henry Clay, who had died eight years earlier. It had been installed in a pavilion at the Virginia state capitol. The former president paid tribute to the renowned senator who had led the Whig effort to impeach him. Tyler was gracious, but he admitted, "doubtless some of the bruises and scars which they inflicted remain to the present day."

PEACE CONFERENCE

In February 1861, Tyler was back in Washington, D.C. This time it was to preside over a peace conference to try to prevent war between the North and the South. Representatives of thirteen northern and seven border states attended. The conference had three main goals: to ban

*In 1860 Tyler addressed a gathering to honor the marble statue of Henry Clay
(right) created by Kentucky sculptor Joel T. Hart for the Ladies' Clay
Association. The statue had been installed in a pavilion (left) on the
grounds of the Virginia state capitol in Richmond in late 1859.*

———————————— ✧ ————————————

slavery north of the Missouri border, to allow slavery south
of that line, and to let new states decide whether they
would allow slavery.

The former president hoped to use his influence with
fellow southerners to avoid a war. By February 28, before
the peace conference ended, Tyler came out in support of
secession. In threatening secession, Southerners wanted to
break away from the United States if the federal government didn't allow them to continue to own slaves.
Southerners feared that the recent election of Abraham
Lincoln, a Northerner, as president would lead to the end
of slavery. Lincoln's election depressed Tyler, who wrote, "I

fear that we have fallen on evil times and that the day of doom for the great model republic is at hand." Like many southerners, Tyler depended on slaves to work his estate. In 1845 he had thirty slaves. At the start of the Civil War (1861–1865), he owned forty-nine.

"RUIN AND DESOLATION WILL PREVAIL"

John Tyler sided with his home state of Virginia when it chose to go to war against the North. But the former president was not optimistic about the South's chance of winning. He realized the North had more money and resources and would eventually win.

Tyler wrote privately to friends and publicly to the *Richmond Enquirer* about what he thought would happen in the Civil War: "The conqueror will walk at every step over smouldering ashes and beneath crumbled columns. States once proud and independent will no longer exist and the glory of the Union will have departed forever. Ruin and desolation will everywhere prevail [be present], and the victors' brow, instead of a wreath of glorious evergreen such as a patriot wear[s], will be encircled with withered and faded leaves bedewed [wet] with the blood of the child and its mother and the father and the son. The picture is too horrible and revolting to be dwelt upon."

Abraham Lincoln's
inauguration as U.S.
president in 1861 spurred
some southern states to
secede from the Union.
──────────── ✧

Abraham Lincoln's inauguration as U.S. president in 1861 spurred some southern states to secede from the Union.

Lincoln took office on March 4, 1861. Soon after, South Carolina, ready to secede, wanted control of Fort Sumter, the federal fort in Charleston harbor. South Carolina prevented Union ships from supplying the fort. When Lincoln finally sent another supply ship, southern troops opened fire on the fort on April 12. The next day, the fort surrendered, and the Civil War was underway.

The Southern states set up a government called the Confederacy. On May 5, Tyler stunned many people in the North by accepting a seat in the Confederacy's Provisional Congress. As the Confederacy established itself, it created a permanent Congress. In November 1861, Tyler won a seat in the Confederate House of Representatives. He is the only former president to serve in the Confederacy. As such, he is the only former president who tried to overthrow the government that he once led. Tyler even offered to carry a musket (gun) and fight for his native Virginia against the North.

*Tyler attended meetings of the Confederate House of Representatives in
the Richmond capitol of the Confederacy. It had been the state capitol
building before the Civil War, and it became the state capitol
again after the war ended in 1865.*

---◇---

In January 1862, Tyler went to Richmond to prepare
for his new role as a Confederate congressman. Back at
their Sherwood Forest home, Julia had a dream that her
husband would die. She rushed to Richmond. Two days
later, on January 12, John Tyler suffered a stroke. He died
on January 18, 1862.

Because the country was at war, Tyler's death attracted
little attention from the North. But the South paused to
honor the seventy-one-year-old leader. His body was laid
out in the Virginia House of Delegates. The funeral proces-
sion included the governor of Virginia, and the president,
vice president, and cabinet of the Confederacy. A fellow

Virginia statesman, William Rives, told Julia that "President Tyler has had the great happiness accorded him of living to see himself fully appreciated. All (Whig) party feelings have faded away, and his old enemies are among his warmest friends." John Tyler is buried in Richmond, next to another former president, James Monroe.

During the Civil War, Union soldiers took over Tyler's Sherwood Forest home. After the war, the mansion became a school for children, both black and white. It wasn't until 1915, more than half a century after his death, that the federal government placed a memorial to President John Tyler at his grave.

He had been known at first as the accidental president, a leader who took over the office of the White House upon the death of President William Henry Harrison. By the time he died, John Tyler was known as a traitor in the North and a hero in the South. His presidency is remembered for its precedent—that the vice president does indeed have the right to assume the full office of the president—and for a catchy campaign slogan: Tippecanoe and Tyler Too. In a way, the slogan ended up being prophetic—Tyler, too, would become president.

TIMELINE

1790   John Tyler is born in Charles City County, Virginia, on March 29.

1807   Tyler graduates from the College of William and Mary.

1808   Tyler receives law degree and begins practicing law.

1810   Voters elect Tyler to the Virginia House of Delegates.

1813   Tyler and Letitia Christian marry on March 29, his twenty-third birthday.

1816   Tyler is elected to the U.S. House of Representatives.

1823   Tyler wins a seat in the Virginia House of Delegates.

1824   Virginia legislators elect Tyler governor.

1827   Virginia legislators elect Tyler U.S. senator.

1836   Tyler resigns his Senate seat and goes home to Virginia.

1838   Voters once again give Tyler a seat in the Virginia House of Delegates.

1839   Whigs choose Tyler to be their vice-presidential candidate.

1840   William Henry Harrison and John Tyler are elected president and vice president, respectively.

1841   Harrison dies on April 4. Tyler is sworn in as president on April 6. Tyler vetoes a Whig plan for a national bank on August 16 and vetoes an amended bank bill on September 9. All but one of Tyler's cabinet resigns on September 11. Whigs expel Tyler from the party on September 13.

1842   The president's daughter Elizabeth marries at the White House on January 31. On February 23, Henry Clay announces plans to resign from the Senate and to run for president. Congress ratifies the Treaty of Washington with

Great Britain, settling the Maine–Canada border dispute on August 20. First Lady Letitia Tyler dies on September 10. Whigs lose heavily to the Democrats in the November congressional elections. Tyler extends the Monroe Doctrine to Hawaii on December 31, providing protection from European colonization.

1843 On January 10, the House of Representatives votes against impeaching President Tyler.

1844 The Peacemaker cannon explodes killing eight men, including two cabinet officers on February 28. On April 22, Tyler asks Congress to ratify the treaty to annex Texas. The Senate rejects the Texas treaty on June 8. Tyler secretly weds Julia Gardiner on June 26. Tyler gives up his reelection bid on August 22. Voters elect Democrat James Polk to be the eleventh president on November 12. On December 3, Tyler again asks Congress to annex Texas.

1845 The Senate passes a resolution to annex Texas on February 27. The House approves the same resolution on February 28. On March 1, Tyler signs the resolution to annex Texas. Polk is sworn in as president on March 4. John and Julia Tyler go home to Virginia on March 5.

1860 Lincoln is elected president. War between the North and the South looms.

1861 Tyler organizes a peace convention of twenty states on February 4. On February 28, Tyler recommends Virginia secede from the Union. The Civil War begins at Fort Sumter, South Carolina, on April 12. Tyler accepts a seat in the Confederacy's Provisional Congress on May 5. Tyler is elected to the Confederacy's permanent Congress in November.

1862 Seventy-one-year-old John Tyler dies in Richmond on January 18, shortly before the Confederate Congress is to begin session.

SOURCE NOTES

7   Philip B. Kunhardt Jr., Philip B. Kunhardt III, and Peter W. Kunhardt, *The American President* (New York: Riverhead Books, 1999), 24.

7   Webb Garrison and Beth Wieder, *A Treasury of White House Tales* (Nashville: Rutledge Hill Press, 2002), 170.

7   Ibid.

7   Ibid.

8   Ibid.

9   Ibid., 172.

9   William W. Freehling, *The Road to Disunion: Secessionists at Bay* (New York: Oxford University Press, 1990), 363.

10 Oliver Perry Chitwood, *John Tyler: Champion of the Old South* (Newtown, CT: American Political Biography Press, 1939), 71.

11–12   Ibid., 10.

12 Ibid., 13.

13 Ibid.

13 Ibid., 12.

14 Ibid., 15.

17 Ibid., 35.

17 Ibid., 44.

18 Ibid., 58.

20 Michael Beschloss, ed., *American Heritage Illustrated History of the Presidents* (New York: Crown Publishers, 2000), 120.

21 Frederick S. Voss, *Portraits of the Presidents: The National Portrait Gallery* (New York: Rizzoli International Publications, Inc., 2000), 39.

29 Kunhardt, Kunhardt, and Kunhardt, 21.

29 Beschloss, 126.

30 Voss, 42.

30 Norma Lois Peterson, *The Presidencies of William Henry Harrison and John Tyler* (Lawrence: University Press of Kansas, 1989), 29.

31 Roger A. Fischer, *Tippecanoe and Trinkets Too: The Material Culture of American Presidential Elections, 1812–1984* (Urbana: University of Illinois Press, 1988), 30.

32 Ibid., 68.

32 Ibid., 30.

33 Beschloss, 125.

35–36   Kunhardt, Kunhardt, and Kunhardt, 21.

36 Ibid.

36 Ibid.

38 Beschloss, 133.

39 Kunhardt, Kunhardt, and Kunhardt, 212.

39 Peterson, 45.

39–40   Kunhardt, Kunhardt, and Kundhardt, 212.

40–41   Ibid.

42 Ibid., 206.

42 Paul C. Light, *Vice-Presidential Power: Advice and Influence in the White House* (Baltimore: The Johns Hopkins University Press, 1984), 7.

43 Tim Taylor, The Book of Presidents (New York: Arno Press, 1972), 645.

45 Carl Sferrazza Anthony, *America's First Families: An Inside View of Two Hundred Years of Private Life in the White House* (New York: Simon & Schuster, 2000), 153.

46 Ibid., 184.

47 Ibid., 153.

47 Ibid.

47 Peterson, 149.
47 Ibid., 148.
47 Ibid., 149.
48 Charles Dickens, *American Notes: A Journey* (1842; repr., New York: Fromm International Publishing Company, 1985), 123.
48 Garrison and Wieder, 40.
49 Dickens, 124–125.
50 Peterson, 60.
50 Ibid., 58.
51–52 Kunhardt, Kunhardt, and Kunhardt, 215.
52 Peterson, 1.
55 Ibid., 78.
57 Kunhardt, Kunhardt, and Kunhardt, 212.
58 Beschloss, 138.
59 Peterson, 168.
59 Ibid.
60 Ibid., 90.
60–61 Ibid.
61 Kunhardt, Kunhardt, and Kunhardt, 212.
63 Peterson, 95.
63 Ibid.
63–64 Ibid., 267.
64 Ibid.
64 Kunhardt, Kunhardt, and Kunhardt, 215.
64 Peterson, 105.
65 Rose Blue and Corrine J. Nader, *Who's That in the White House? The Formative Years, 1829–1857* (Austin, TX: Raintree Steck-Vaughn Co., 1998), 48.
66 Peterson, 130.
66 Ibid.
66 Ibid.
66 Ibid., 112.
67 Kunhardt, Kunhardt, and Kunhardt, 214.
68–69 Peterson, 167.
70 Ibid., 147.
70 Ibid.
70 Taylor, 640.
71 Peterson, 106.

72 Garrison and Wieder, 23.
72 Freehling, 391.
73 Beschloss, 138.
73 Garrison and Wieder, 22.
74 Ibid., 23.
75 Ibid.
75 Paul F. Boller Jr., *Presidential Wives: An Anecdotal History* (New York: Oxford University Press, 1988), 82.
76 Anthony, 130.
76 Peterson, 228.
80 Boller, 82.
80 Ibid., 83.
80 Garrison and Wieder, 208.
80 Peterson, 237.
81 Anthony, 267.
81 Ibid., 130.
82 Ibid.
82 Ibid.
82 Boller, 84.
83 Anthony, 301.
85 Peterson, 232.
87 Kunhardt, Kunhardt, and Kunhardt, 215.
88 Beschloss, 139.
89 Peterson, 238.
90 Ibid., 239.
90 Beschloss, 137.
92 Boller, 83.
92 Marc W. Kruman, "John Tyler," in *The Reader's Companion to the American Presidency*, eds., Alan Brinkley and Davis Dyer (Boston: Houghton Mifflin Co., 2000), 139.
93 Kunhardt, Kunhardt, and Kundardt, 212.
97 Chitwood, 412.
97 Ibid., 413.
98 Ibid., 425.
98 Ibid.
99–100 Ibid., 440.
100 Ibid.
103 Ibid., 442.

SELECTED BIBLIOGRAPHY

Beschloss, Michael, ed. *American Heritage Illustrated History of the Presidents*. New York: Crown Publishers, 2000.

Boller, Paul F., Jr. *Presidential Wives: An Anecdotal History*. New York: Oxford University Press, 1988.

Brinkley, Alan, and Davis Dyer, eds. *The Reader's Companion to the American Presidency*. Boston: Houghton Mifflin Co., 2000.

Chitwood, Oliver Perry. *John Tyler: Champion of the Old South*. Newtown, CT: American Political Biography Press, 1939.

Dickens, Charles. *American Notes: A Journey*, 1842. Reprint, New York: Fromm International Publishing Company, 1985.

Fischer, Roger A. *Tippecanoe and Trinkets Too: The Material Culture of American Presidential Elections, 1812–1984*. Urbana: University of Illinois Press, 1988.

Freehling, William W. *The Road to Disunion: Secessionists at Bay*. New York: Oxford University Press, 1990.

Frey, Marc, and Todd Davis. *The New Big Book of U.S. Presidents*. Philadelphia: Running Press, 2000.

Garrison, Webb, and Beth Wieder. *A Treasury of White House Tales*. Nashville: Rutledge Hill Press, 2002.

Grant, Ulysses S. *Memoirs and Selected Letters: Personal Memoirs of U. S. Grant/Selected Letters 1839–1865*. Edited by Mary McFeely and William S. McFeely. New York: Library of America, 1990.

Kunhardt, Philip B., Jr., Philip B. Kunhardt III, and Peter W. Kunhardt. *The American President*. New York: Riverhead Books, 1999.

Light, Paul C. *Vice-Presidential Power: Advice and Influence in the White House*. Baltimore: The Johns Hopkins University Press, 1984.

McPherson, James M., ed. *To the Best of My Ability: The American Presidents*. New York: Dorling Kindersley, 2000.

Pessen, Edward. *The Log Cabin Myth: The Social Backgrounds of the Presidents*. New Haven, CT: Yale University Press, 1984.

Peterson, Norma Lois. *The Presidencies of William Henry Harrison and John Tyler*. Lawrence: University Press of Kansas, 1989.

FURTHER READING AND WEBSITES

American Presidents, Life Portraits
http://www.americanpresidents.org
This is C-SPAN's web companion to its series of U.S. presidents. Included is a brief biography and portrait of John Tyler.

Anthony, Carl Sferrazza. *America's First Families: An Inside View of Two Hundred Years of Private Life in the White House.* New York: Simon & Schuster, 2000.

Behrman, Carol H. *Andrew Jackson.* Minneapolis: Lerner Publications Company, 2003.

———. *James K. Polk.* Minneapolis: Lerner Publications Company, 2005.

Blue, Rose, and Corrine J. Nader. *Who's That in the White House? The Formative Years, 1829–1857.* Austin, TX: Raintree Steck-Vaughn Co., 1998.

Humes, James. *Which President Killed a Man? Tantalizing Trivia and Fun Facts About Our Chief Executives and First Ladies.* Chicago: Contemporary Books, 2003.

John Tyler's Home, Sherwood Forest
http://www.sherwoodforest.org
The website includes a virtual tour of Sherwood Forest, owned by the president's grandson, information on the ghost that haunts the house, and a brief biography of John Tyler.

Lazo, Caroline Evenson. *Martin Van Buren.* Minneapolis: Lerner Publications Company, 2005.

The Official White House Website
http://www.whitehouse.gov/history/
This site includes a tour of the White House and biographies and portraits of all the presidents.

Voss, Frederick S. *Portraits of the Presidents: The National Portrait Gallery.* New York: Rizzoli International Publications, Inc., 2000.

INDEX

ABOUT THE AUTHOR

Kate Havelin was in junior high when she decided to be a writer. She edited her high school and college newspapers and studied journalism. After graduating, she worked as a television producer for more than a decade. This is Havelin's twelfth book for young readers. She lives with her husband and two sons in St. Paul, Minnesota.

❖